# Animal Art of Etosha
# Tierkunst von Etoscha
# Dierekuns van Etosha

## The Legend of Etosha

There is an old Bushman legend about a group of strangers who once strayed into Bushman territory. They were tracked down by a party of hunters who killed all the men and children but allowed the women to go free. One young mother, overcome by grief, sat under a tree, rocking her dead infant in her arms. So copiously did she weep that her tears formed a huge lake, and when the sun had dried the lake, the ground was covered in salt. That, say the Bushmen, is how the Etosha Pan was formed – the lake of a mother's tears.

## Die Etoscha-Legende

Einer alten Buschmann-Legende nach verirrte sich eines Tages eine Gruppe Fremder und gelangte ins Buschmanngebiet. Sie wurden von Jägern umzingelt, die alle Männer und Kinder ums Leben brachten, aber die Frauen freiliessen. Von tiefer Trauer erfüllt, setzte sich eine junge Mutter unter einen Baum und wiegte ihr totes Kind in den Armen. Sie weinte so bitterlich, dass ihre Tränen einen grossen See bildeten. Als die Sonne den See ausgetrocknet hatte, war der Boden mit Salz bedeckt. Die Buschmänner sagen, das sei der Ursprung der Etoschapfanne – des Sees der Tränen einer Mutter.

## Die Legende van Etosha

'n Ou Boesman-legende lui dat 'n groep vreemdelinge eendag afgedwaal en in Boesman-gebied beland het. Jagters het hulle omsingel en al die mans en kinders om die lewe gebring, maar die vroue laat gaan. Onder 'n boom het 'n jong moeder, oorweldig deur smart, haar dooie kind in haar arms gewieg. So bitterlik het sy geween dat haar trane 'n groot meer gevorm het. Toe die son die meer opdroog, was die grond met sout bedek. Dít, sê die Boesmans, is die oorsprong van Etoshapan – die meer van 'n moeder se trane.

All profits derived from the sale of this publication
will go towards the conservation of our wildlife.

Der Erlös aus dem Verkauf dieser Publikation
wird zur Erhaltung unserer Naturschutzgebiete angewendet.

Alle wins wat hierdie publikasie oplewer,
sal aangewend word vir die bewaring van ons natuurlewe.

# Animal Art of Etosha
# Tierkunst von Etoscha
# Dierekuns van Etosha

Department of Agriculture and Nature Conservation, South West Africa/Namibia, in collaboration with the Southern African Nature Foundation – member of the World Wildlife Fund.

Abteilung für Landwirtschaft und Naturschutz, Südwestafrika/Namibia, in Zusammenarbeit mit der Stiftung für Naturschutz, Südliches Afrika – Mitglied des Welt-Naturschutzfonds.

Departement van Landbou en Natuurbewaring, Suidwes-Afrika/Namibië, in medewerking met die Suider-Afrikaanse Natuurstigting – lid van die Wêreldnatuurfonds.

First published in 1986 by
The Department of Agriculture and Nature Conservation
Directorate of Nature Conservation and Recreation Resorts
Private Bag 13306
9000 WINDHOEK
South West Africa/Namibia
in collaboration with
The S.A. Nature Foundation
P.O. Box 456
7600 STELLENBOSCH
Republic of South Africa

ISBN  0  620  09715  9




Design by Philip Smuts
Lithographic reproduction and typesetting
by Hirt & Carter, Cape Town
Printed and bound by
National Book Printers, Goodwood, Cape

**Cover illustration:**  Zakkie Eloff:  Etosha Pan, pen-and-wash, 69 x 31,5 cm

## Foreword

On the occasion of the re-opening of the Namutoni rest camp in Etosha in August, 1984, the President of the Southern African Nature Foundation, Dr. Anton Rupert, apropos a conversation with Dr. Willie van Niekerk, former Administrator-General, broached the possibility of publishing a selection from the works of wildlife artists of Etosha. The idea was that it would not only stimulate interest in our wildlife, but would also make a real contribution to nature conservation.

This idea has now been realised through the efforts of Dr. Rupert. The department is deeply grateful to him for his inspiration and support, without which this publication would not have been possible.

**Animal Art of Etosha** is also a tribute to all artists who through their sensitive portrayal of wildlife have made an important contribution towards promoting a wider awareness and appreciation of our rich natural heritage.

I trust that all those who acquire this book will derive great pleasure from the beauty and splendour of our large variety of wild animals.

A.Z. SHIPANGA
Minister of Nature Conservation, Mining, Commerce and Tourism
South West Africa/Namibia

## Vorwort

Als im August 1984 die Raststätte Namutoni in der Etoschapfanne wiedereröffnet wurde, wies Dr. Anton Rupert, der Präsident der Stiftung für Naturschutz, Südliches Afrika, anlässlich eines Gesprächs mit Dr. Willie van Niekerk, dem ehemaligen General-Administrator, auf die Möglichkeit hin, eine Auswahl aus den Werken der Maler zu publizieren, die Tiere der Etoschapfanne gemalt haben. Dadurch werde nicht nur das Interesse an unseren Naturschutzgebieten gefördert, sondern auch ein Beitrag zu ihrer Erhaltung geleistet.

Mit der Hilfe von Dr. Rupert konnte diese Idee nun verwirklicht werden. Das Ministerium schuldet ihm grossen Dank für seine Anregung und Unterstützung, ohne die diese Publikation nicht hätte erscheinen können.

**Tierkunst von Etoscha** ist gleichzeitig eine Huldigung der Künstler, die mit ihren feinfühligen Darstellungen des Tierlebens zu einem stärkeren Umweltbewusstsein und zur Erhaltung unseres reichen Naturerbes sehr viel beigetragen haben.

Ich hoffe, dass alle, die dieses Buch in die Hand nehmen, Freude an der Schönheit und Vielfalt unserer wilden Tiere haben werden.

A.Z. SHIPANGA
Minister für Naturschutz, Bergbau, Handel und Fremdenverkehr
Südwestafrika/Namibia

## Voorwoord

By die heropening van Namutoni-ruskamp in Etosha in Augustus 1984 het die president van die Suider-Afrikaanse Natuurstigting, dr. Anton Rupert, na aanleiding van 'n gesprek met dr. Willie van Niekerk, voormalige administrateur-generaal, die moontlikheid aangeroer om 'n keur uit die werk van dierekunstenaars van Etosha te publiseer. Dít sou nie net die belangstelling in ons natuurlewe aanwakker nie, maar ook 'n bydrae lewer tot die beskerming daarvan.

Deur bemiddeling van dr. Rupert is hierdie ideaal nou verwesenlik, en die departement is hom innig dankbaar vir sy inspirasie en ondersteuning. Daarsonder sou hierdie publikasie nie moontlik gewees het nie.

**Dierekuns van Etosha** is terselfdertyd 'n huldeblyk aan die kunstenaars van ons natuurlewe wat met hul sensitiewe uitbeeldings 'n belangrike bydrae maak ter bevordering van 'n groter omgewings-bewustheid en die bewaring van ons ryke natuurerfenis.

Ek vertrou dat almal wat hierdie boek opneem, opnuut genot en verkwikking sal put uit die bekoring en prag van ons groot verskeidenheid wilde diere.

A.Z. SHIPANGA
Minister van Natuurbewaring, Mynbou, Handel en Toerisme
Suidwes-Afrika/Namibië

## Acknowledgements

The publishers wish to thank the following for their valuable contributions:

The artists and owners for granting permission to have their works reproduced;

Hilda Wasserfall of Windhoek for locating and selecting the works of art and for supplying the biographical data of the artists;

Adelheid Lilienthal of Windhoek for writing the introduction;

Nana Wagner of Stellenbosch for her cordial assistance and advice;

Lieschen Heinze of the Chelsea Gallery in Wynberg, Cape Town, for her assistance with regard to the work of Johannes Blatt;

Peter Strack of Windhoek for his assistance in respect of the work of Fritz Krampe;

the Arts Association of SWA/Namibia for friendly assistance;

Uschi Oldorf and Heidemarie Rapmund of the Kunstkabinett, Windhoek, for assistance regarding the etchings of Heinz Pulon.

## Dankesworte

Die Herausgeber danken den Folgenden für ihre wertvollen Beiträge:

Den Künstlern und Eigentümern der Kunstwerke für die Erlaubnis der Wiedergabe;

Hilda Wasserfall aus Windhoek, die die Werke aufgespürt, ausgewählt und die biographischen Angaben zu den Künstlern geliefert hat;

Adelheid Lilienthal aus Windhoek, die die Einleitung verfasst hat;

Nana Wagner aus Stellenbosch für ihren Rat und ihre freundliche Hilfe;

Lieschen Heinze von der Chelsea-Galerie in Wynberg, Kapstadt, für ihre Hilfe im Zusammenhang mit den Werken von Johannes Blatt;

Peter Strack aus Windhoek für seine Hilfe im Zusammenhang mit den Werken von Fritz Krampe;

der Kunstvereinigung von SWA/Namibia für ihre freundliche Hilfe;

Uschi Oldorf und Heidemarie Rapmund vom Kunstkabinett in Windhoek für Hilfeleistung im Zusammenhang mit den Radierungen von Heinz Pulon.

## Dankbetuiging

Die uitgewers spreek graag hul dank uit teenoor die volgende vir hul gewaardeerde bydrae:

Die kunstenaars en eienaars vir toestemming om hul werke te reproduseer;

Hilda Wasserfall van Windhoek vir die opspoor en keuring van die kunswerke en vir die voorsiening van die biografiese besonderhede van die kunstenaars;

Adelheid Lilienthal van Windhoek vir die skryf van die inleidingsartikel;

Nana Wagner van Stellenbosch vir haar welwillende hulp en advies;

Lieschen Heinze van die Chelsea-galery in Wynberg, Kaapstad, vir haar hulp in verband met die werke van Johannes Blatt;

Peter Strack van Windhoek vir sy hulp ten opsigte van die werke van Fritz Krampe;

die Kunsvereniging van SWA/Namibië vir vriendelike hulp verleen;

Uschi Oldorf en Heidemarie Rapmund van die Kunstkabinett, Windhoek, vir hulp in verband met die etse van Heinz Pulon.

# Contents     Inhalt     Inhoud

## Introduction

### ANIMALS IN THE ART OF AFRICA

Early man viewed animals – because of their natural means of defence and special characteristics – as dangerous opponents of equal standing, to be treated with circumspection and reverence; as somewhat mysterious creatures, and yet possessed of a soul. In his art animals are depicted not only as quarry, but also as symbolic figures, and in the sphere of religious worship and cults, as images endowed with supernatural powers.

Examples of these conceptions are found in the early art forms of all peoples and continents, but especially in Africa, a continent abounding in wildlife.

In prehistoric rock art, man's oldest art form, and particularly in the so-called "Bushman paintings" of Southern Africa, images of animals serve as a talisman to the hunter, promoting fertility and ritual magic. In Bushman myth, where man and animal are interchangeable, many tales begin with the line: "Once upon a time, when animals were people..." Even though the origin, age and purpose of rock art have not yet been fully determined, the freshness and beauty of these animal images, which are between ten and twenty thousand years old, still enchant us today.

In the ancient Egyptian cult of the dead, over four thousand years ago, animals were depicted not only as quarry, as domesticated beasts or in hieroglyphic form, but also – when combined with the

## Einleitung

### DAS TIER IN DER KUNST AFRIKAS

Der Mensch früherer Jahrhunderte empfand das Tier, wegen seiner natürlichen Waffen und ausgeprägten Eigenarten, als gefährlichen Gegner und gleichwertiges Gegenüber, dem mit Vorsicht und in Ehrfurcht zu begegnen war. Als ein nicht ganz deutbares und doch beseeltes Wesen der Schöpfung, wurde es in der Kunst nicht nur als Jagdbeute dargestellt, sondern auch als Symbolfigur und Abbild überweltlicher Mächte im religiösen und kultischen Bereich.

Beispiele dieser Sehensweise finden sich in der frühzeitlichen Kunst aller Völker und Kontinente, doch besonders in Afrika, einem Erdteil vielfältigen Wildreichtums.

In der ältesten Kunst der Menschheit, der prähistorischen Felsmalerei, und besonders in der sog. "Buschmannmalerei" des südlichen Afrikas dient der Tierkörper dem Jagdglück, der Fruchtbarkeit, dem rituellen Zauber. Nach dem Buschmannmythos sind Mensch und Tier austauschbar, beginnen viele Märchen mit dem Satz: "Das Tier, welches früher ein Mensch gewesen ist..." Obwohl Ursprung, Alter und Zweck der Felsmalerei noch nicht ganz enträtselt sind, bezaubern noch heute Lebensnähe und Schönheit dieser zehn- bis zwanzigtausend Jahre alten Tierfiguren.

Im Totenkult Ägyptens, vor über viertausend Jahren, wird das Tier nicht nur als Jagdbeute, Nutztier und Schriftzeichen dargestellt, sondern erlangt, in der

## Inleiding

### DIE DIER IN DIE KUNS VAN AFRIKA

In vroeëre eeue het die mens die dier, met sy natuurlike wapens en sy besondere eienskappe, beskou as 'n gevaarlike en gelykwaardige teëstander wat met ontsag en eerbied bejeën moes word. Vir hom was die dier ietwat geheimsinnig, maar nogtans 'n wese met 'n siel. Daarom het hy dit in sy kuns nie net as jagbuit voorgestel nie, maar ook as simboliese figuur, en as 'n beeld van boaardse magte in die religieuse en kultiese sfeer.

Ons vind voorbeelde van hierdie sienswyse in die vroeë kuns van alle volke en vastelande, maar veral in Afrika met sy talryke wildsoorte.

In die mens se oudste kunsvorm, die prehistoriese rotstekeninge, en veral in die sogenaamde "Boesmantekeninge" van Suider-Afrika, hou die afbeelding van diere verband met welslae op jagtogte, met vrugbaarheid en die rituele toorkuns. In die Boesman-mitologie is mens en dier uitruilbaar. Talle sprokies begin met die woorde: "Die dier, wat vroeër 'n mens was..." Hoewel die oorsprong, ouderdom en doel van die rotstekeninge nog nie heeltemal ontraaisel is nie, bly die lewensgetrouheid en skoonheid van hierdie dierefigure ná tien- tot twintigduisend jaar steeds bekoorlik.

Meer as vierduisend jaar gelede is die dier in Egipte se dodekultus nie net as jagbuit, huisdier of skrifteken uitgebeeld nie maar ook, in verbintenis met die mens, as 'n

image of man – as beings endowed with divine omnipotence. Thus the king-god Horus is shown with a falcon's head on a human body.

Magical thought has shaped African tribal art. Magic means the ability to influence and possibly change the course of nature. Animals endue man with secret powers that increase fertility and physical strength and appease the spirits. Before the hunt, the artist casts his spell over his potential quarry by painting and carving it.
Sculptures of wood, bronze, clay and stone, as well as totems, fetishes and masks are still made today for similar reasons.

In Europe art developed over centuries. The European artists who worked creatively in Southern Africa during the 19th and 20th centuries were therefore equipped with valuable experience and stylistic resources, which they combined with African themes and colours.

As epochs passed, the significance of animals in European art changed, and so did the relationship between man and animal. The magical meaning of animal images is amply evident in the ornamentations of the Germanic tribes and even in early Christian art. All art styles of the Middle Ages attribute to animals a symbolic meaning in the form of good and evil. Out of this symbolism heraldry evolved. During the 15th century the mystical relationship between man and animal was brought to an end by the Renaissance and the scientific exploration of the world, by man's increased self-awareness and the invention of new hunting weapons. In

Verbindung mit dem Menschen, göttliche Allmacht: so trägt Königsgott Horus einen Falkenkopf auf menschlicher Gestalt.

Magisches Denken bestimmt die Stammeskunst Afrikas. Magie ist die Gabe, den Naturablauf zu beeinflussen und möglicherweise zu ändern. Das Tier verleiht dem Menschen hierzu geheimnisvolle Kräfte, die die Fruchtbarkeit erhöhen, die Körperkräfte stärken, die Geister besänftigen. Der Künstler, der das zu jagende Tier malend und schnitzend einfängt, zwingt es in seinen Bann.
In diesem Sinne entstehen noch heute Plastiken aus Holz, Bronze, Ton und Stein, Totems, Fetische und Masken.

Europäische Künstler, die im 19. und 20. Jahrhundert im südlichen Afrika schöpferisch tätig wurden, brachten Erfahrungswerte und stilistische Mittel einer jahrhundertealten Kunstentwicklung aus Europa mit und verbanden sie mit afrikanischer Thematik und Farbgebung.

In der Kunst Europas wandelte sich im Laufe der Epochen die Bedeutung des Tieres in der Kunst, so wie auch das Verhältnis zwischen Mensch und Tier sich änderte. Die Tierornamentik der Germanen, selbst noch die frühchristliche Kunst, vermitteln beredtes Zeugnis von der magischen Bedeutung des Tieres. Durch alle Stile des Mittelalters wird dem Tier, in der Verkörperung des Guten und Bösen, symbolische Bedeutung zuteil, woraus sich auch die Heraldik entwickelte. Erst durch die Renaissance, die wissenschaftliche Erforschung der Welt, die Stärkung des Ich-Bewusstseins des Menschen und die

goddelike mag: die menslike gestalte van die koningsgod Horus dra byvoorbeeld die kop van 'n valk.

Afrika se stamkuns word gerig deur magiese denke. Magiese krag is die vermoë om natuurgebeure te beïnvloed en dalk selfs te verander. Daarvoor verleen die dier aan die mens geheimsinnige kragte wat sy vrugbaarheid verhoog, sy liggaam versterk, en die geeste besweer. Die kunstenaar wat sy beoogde prooi in sy tekening of houtsneewerk verbeeld, kry daardeur beheer oor die dier. Om hierdie rede word beelde uit hout, brons, klei en klip, asook totems, fetisje en maskers, vandag nog gemaak.

Europese kunstenaars wat in die negentiende en twintigste eeu in Suider-Afrika hul kuns beoefen het, het die ervaring en stilistiese middele van 'n eeue-oue kunsontwikkeling uit Europa saamgebring en dit verbind met temas en kleure wat eie is aan Afrika.

Die betekenis van die dier in die Europese kuns het deur die eeue verander, en so ook die verhouding tussen mens en dier. Die dier-ornamentiek van die Germane, en selfs nog die kuns van die vroeë Christendom, getuig duidelik van die dier se magiese betekenis. In alle Middeleeuse stylvorme kry die dier in die vergestalting van Goed en Kwaad 'n simboliese betekenis, en daaruit het later die heraldiek ontwikkel. Eers in die vyftiende eeu maak die Renaissance, die wetenskaplike ontdekking van die wêreld, die mens se verhoogde selfbewussyn, en die uitvinding van nuwe jagwapens 'n

subsequent developments in European art up to the 20th century, animals were characterised according to the prevailing tastes of the various periods, or fascinated painters, sculptors and graphic artists purely with their physical appearance and aesthetic form.

In the relatively young art of South West Africa/Namibia, where European influence is strongly evident, animals are seldom depicted symbolically. In our technological and hectic times, wildlife and its environment are above all cherished as the natural and the unspoilt, and as a refuge for the soul. All predominantly naturalistic art works express a love of animals, of their grace, strength and beauty. European and traditional African art styles have so far neither affected each other nor merged, nor is it possible, in the present stage of development, to discern an overall Namibian art style.

In a country like South West Africa/Namibia, where conservation of its rich wildlife is an established practice, and where the observation of game in its natural surroundings is one of the great attractions, animals as subject matter in art will continue to exist, regardless of stylistic or interpretative trends.

Erfindung neuer Jagdwaffen, findet die mystische Beziehung zwischen Mensch und Tier im 15. Jahrhundert ihr Ende. In der weiteren Kunstentwicklung Europas, bis ins 20. Jahrhundert hinein, dient das Tier der Wiedergabe des Zeitgefühls oder fasziniert Maler, Bildhauer und Grafiker wegen seiner rein körperlichen Erscheinung, seiner ästhetischen Formgebung.

Auch in der noch jungen, europäisch geprägten Kunst Südwestafrikas/Namibias kommt dem Tier selten symbolhafte Bedeutung zu, das Wild und seine Umgebung wird, in unserem technisierten, hektischen Zeitalter, vielmehr als seelisches Refugium, als Quelle des Natürlichen, Ursprünglichen verehrt. In allen vorwiegend naturalistischen Kunstwerken drückt sich die Liebe zum Tier, zur Anmut, Kraft und Schönheit seines Körpers aus. Die Begegnung europäischer und traditioneller afrikanischer Kunststile und deren Verschmelzung hat noch nicht stattgefunden, ebensowenig wie man zu diesem Zeitpunkt von einem allgemeinen, eigenständigen namibianischen künstlerischen Ausdruck sprechen kann.

In einem Land wie Südwestafrika/Namibia, in dem es die Tierhege des reichen Wildbestandes gibt, und die Tierbeobachtung in freier Wildbahn zu den grossen Attraktionen zählt, wird das Tier als künstlerisches Thema weiterhin bestehen, in welcher Stilrichtung und in welchem Sinngehalt auch immer.

einde aan die mistiese verhouding tussen mens en dier. In die verdere Europese kunsontwikkeling tot in die twintigste eeu word die dier gebruik om die tydgees weer te gee, of besiel dit skilders, beeldhouers en grafiese kunstenaars bloot met sy gestalte en sy estetiese vorm.

Ook in die nog jong, Europees-geskoolde kuns van Suidwes-Afrika/Namibië dra die dier selde 'n simboliese betekenis. In ons tegnologiese, gejaagde tyd word wilde diere en hul omgewing veeleer as geestelike toevlugsoord vereer, as bronwel van die natuurlike en argetipiese. Al dié oorwegend naturalistiese kunswerke verbeeld die liefde vir die dier en sy grasie, krag en skoonheid. Daar was nog geen ontmoeting of samesmelting tussen die Europese en tradisionele Afrika-kunsstyle nie, en van 'n algemene, eiesoortige Namibiese kunsstyl kan daar nog geen sprake wees nie.

In 'n land soos Suidwes-Afrika/Namibië, waar bewaring op die talryke wildsoorte toegepas word en waar wild in die vrye natuur 'n groot besienswaardigheid is, sal die dier steeds 'n kunstema bly, ongeag stylrigtings of opvattings.

ADELHEID LILIENTHAL
Past Vice-President
Arts Association of SWA/Namibia

ADELHEID LILIENTHAL
Ehemalige Vizepräsidentin
Kunstvereinigung von SWA/Namibia

ADELHEID LILIENTHAL
Voormalige vise-presidente
Kunsvereniging van SWA/Namibië

## Dieter Aschenborn

Dieter Aschenborn was born in Okahandja in 1915. At the age of five he accompanied his father, the artist Hans Anton Aschenborn, to Germany, where he received his school education. As a young boy he had his first training in art from his father, but he is predominantly a self-taught artist.

Aschenborn was assistant game-warden in Etosha for two years and later frequently led safaris. He is known especially for his decorative wooden panels, stamp designs and book illustrations. His water-colours show technical skill and acute perception. His main interest lies in the more decorative visual aspects of wildlife.

Dieter Aschenborn wurde 1915 in Okahandja geboren. Als Fünfjähriger begleitete er seinen Vater, den Künstler Hans Anton Aschenborn, nach Deutschland, wo er die Schule besuchte. Den anfänglichen Kunstunterricht empfing er als Kind von seinem Vater, doch abgesehen davon ist er hauptsächlich Autodidakt.

Zwei Jahre lang war er Hilfswildhüter in der Etoschapfanne und später leitete er des öfteren Safaris. Bekannt wurde er vor allem durch seine dekorativen Holztafeln, seine Briefmarkenentwürfe und Buchillustrationen. Seine Aquarellskizzen zeugen von grosser Geschicklichkeit und einer scharfen Beobachtungsgabe. Sein Interesse beschränkt sich vor allem auf die dekorativen visuellen Aspekte des Tierlebens.

Dieter Aschenborn is in 1915 te Okahandja gebore. As vyfjarige vergesel hy sy vader, die kunstenaar Hans Anton Aschenborn, na Duitsland, waar hy sy skoolopleiding ontvang. Afgesien van die aanvanklike kunsonderrig wat hy as jong seun van sy vader gekry het, is hy hoofsaaklik outodidak.

Aschenborn was twee jaar lank assistent-wildbewaarder in Etosha en tree later dikwels op as safari-leier. Hy is veral bekend vir sy dekoratiewe houtpanele, posseëlontwerpe en boekillustrasies. Sy waterverfsketse getuig van vaardigheid en fyn waarnemingsvermoë. Sy belangstelling is hoofsaaklik beperk tot die meer sierlike visuele aspekte van die dierelewe.

Burchell's zebra and foal
Water-colour, 26 x 40 cm
Coll. artist

Steppenzebra und Füllen
Aquarell, 26 x 40 cm
Sammlung Künstler

Bontkwagga en vul
Waterverf, 26 x 40 cm
Vers. kunstenaar

**Blue wildebeest**
Water-colour, 27 x 45 cm
Coll. artist

**Streifengnus**
Aquarell, 27 x 45 cm
Sammlung Künstler

**Blouwildebeeste**
Waterverf, 27 x 45 cm
Vers. kunstenaar

**Kudu**
Pen-and-ink, 20 x 28 cm
Coll. R Kusters, Windhoek

**Kudu**
Federzeichnung, 20 x 28 cm
Sammlung R Kusters, Windhoek

**Koedoes**
Pentekening, 20 x 28 cm
Vers. R Kusters, Windhoek

**Warthogs**
Water-colour, 16 x 32 cm
Coll. artist

**Warzenschweine**
Aquarell, 16 x 32 cm
Sammlung Künstler

**Vlakvarke**
Waterverf, 16 x 32 cm
Vers. kunstenaar

## Johannes Blatt

Johannes Blatt was born in 1905 in Trier, Germany. In 1912 he emigrated with his parents to Swakopmund, S.W.A., and there received his early training in art at Axel Eriksson's studio. In 1921 he returned to Germany and enrolled as an art student at the Schule am Lerchenfeld in Hamburg. Having completed his studies, he settled in Swakopmund from where he made numerous painting trips into the interior, concentrating especially on landscapes and wildlife studies. His romantic and realistic early works include some charming etchings of the smaller animal species. From 1954 until his death in 1972 his work went into a new phase, growing into a vibrant, personal neo-impressionism characterised by brighter colours, fragmented by short, energetic brush strokes, and compositions that verged on the theatrical.

Johannes Blatt wurde 1905 in Trier geboren. 1912 wanderte er mit seinen Eltern nach Swakopmund, S.W.A., aus. Hier bekam er seinen ersten Kunstunterricht im Atelier von Axel Eriksson. 1921 kehrte er nach Deutschland zurück und wurde Kunststudent an der Schule am Lerchenfeld in Hamburg. Nach Beendigung seines Studiums liess er sich in Swakopmund nieder, und von dort aus unternahm er zahlreiche Malexkursionen ins Inland. Er konzentrierte sich vor allem auf Landschaftsmalerei und Tierstudien. Seine frühen Werke haben romantischen und realistischen Charakter. Während dieser Zeit schuf er bezaubernde Radierungen von kleineren Tierarten. 1954 betrat er eine neue Phase, die bis zu seinem Tod im Jahre 1972 dauerte. Sein Stil entwickelte sich zu einem lebenskräftigen, persönlichen Neo-Impressionismus. Die Farben wurden heller, fragmentiert durch kurze, energische Pinselstriche und seine Kompositionen bekamen eine fast theatralische Qualität.

Johannes Blatt is in 1905 in Trier, Duitsland, gebore. In 1912 emigreer hy saam met sy ouers na Swakopmund, S.W.A., waar hy sy vroeë kunsonderrig in die ateljee van Axel Eriksson ontvang. In 1921 keer hy terug na Duitsland as kunstudent aan die Schule am Lerchenfeld te Hamburg. Ná afloop van sy studie vestig hy hom in Swakopmund, vanwaar hy talle skildertogte na die binneland onderneem. Hy lê hom veral toe op landskapkuns en dierestudies. Sy vroeë werke is romanties en realisties van aard. Gedurende hierdie tydperk maak hy bekoorlike etse van kleiner diersoorte. Van 1954 af betree hy 'n nuwe fase wat duur tot sy dood in 1972. Sy styl ontwikkel tot 'n lewenskragtige, persoonlike neo-impressionisme. Sy kleure word helderder, gefragmenteer deur die gebruik van kort, energieke kwashale, en sy komposisies byna teatraal.

Ostriches
Mixed media, 54 x 114 cm
Coll. K Stern, Windhoek

Strausse
Mischtechnik, 54 x 114 cm
Sammlung K Stern, Windhoek

Volstruise
Gemengde media, 54 x 114 cm
Vers. K Stern, Windhoek

**Steenbok**
Etching, 14 x 9,5 cm
Arts Association of SWA/Namibia

**Steinböckchen**
*Radierung, 14 x 9,5 cm*
*Kunstvereinigung von SWA/Namibia*

**Steenbok**
Ets, 14 x 9,5 cm
Kunsvereniging van SWA/Namibië

**Wild cat**
Etching, 15 x 10,5 cm
Chelsea Gallery, Wynberg, Cape

**Wildkatze**
Radierung, 15 x 10,5 cm
Chelsea-Galerie, Wynberg, Kap

**Wildekat**
Ets, 15 x 10,5 cm
Chelsea-galery, Wynberg, Kaap

**Bat-eared fox**
Etching, 13 x 17 cm
Arts Association of SWA/Namibia

**Löffelhund**
Radierung, 13 x 17 cm
Kunstvereinigung von SWA/Namibia

**Bakoorvos**
Ets, 13 x 17 cm
Kunsvereniging van SWA/Namibië

1930

## Zakkie Eloff

Zakkie Eloff was born on a farm in Botswana in 1925 and received his first art training under Walter Battiss at Pretoria Boys' High School. He continued his studies at the Witwatersrand Technical College under Maurice van Essche and Phyllis Gardner. In 1957 he enrolled at the Central School of Art in London where he studied painting and graphic techniques.
After further studies at various European art centres, he returned to South Africa to take up a teaching post at the Pretoria Technical College. From 1962 to 1968 he was appointed game-warden in Etosha.
He maintains that this stage of his life made an invaluable contribution to his career as a wildlife artist.

Eloff's light-hearted and sometimes humorous approach lends a unique character to his pen-and-wash drawings and is also reflected in the bright colours of his paintings.

Zakkie Eloff wurde 1925 auf einer Farm in Botswana geboren. Seinen ersten Kunstunterricht empfing er von Walter Battiss an der **Pretoria Boys' High School** und am **Witwatersrand Technical College** setzte er sein Studium unter Leitung von Maurice van Essche und Phyllis Gardner fort. 1957 schrieb er sich an der **Central School of Art** in London ein, wo er Malerei und graphische Techniken studierte. Nach weiteren Studien an verschiedenen europäischen Kunstzentren kehrte er nach Südafrika zurück und nahm einen Posten als Dozent am **Pretoria Technical College** an. Von 1962 bis 1968 war er als Wildhüter in der Etoschapfanne tätig. Für ihn lieferte dieser Zeitraum seines Lebens einen wertvollen Beitrag zu seiner Laufbahn als Natur- und Tiermaler.

Eloffs spielerische, manchmal humoristische Einstellung verleiht seinen Feder- und Pinselzeichnungen einen einzigartigen Charakter. Diese Eigenschaft ist auch in den hellen Farben seiner Gemälde reflektiert.

Zakkie Eloff is in 1925 op 'n plaas in Botswana gebore. Hy ontvang sy aanvanklike kunsonderrig aan die Pretoria Boys' High School onder Walter Battiss, en sit sy studie voort aan die Witwatersrandse Tegniese Kollege onder leiding van Maurice van Essche en Phyllis Gardner. In 1957 skryf hy hom in aan die Central School of Art in Londen, waar hy skilderkuns en grafiese tegnieke bestudeer. Ná verdere studie aan verskeie Europese kunssentrums, aanvaar hy by sy terugkeer 'n pos as dosent aan die Pretoriase Tegniese Kollege. Van 1962 tot 1968 was hy wildbewaarder in Etosha. Hy beskou hierdie tydperk van sy lewe as 'n waardevolle bydrae tot sy loopbaan as skilder van die natuurlewe.

Eloff se speelse, soms humoristiese, benadering verleen 'n eiesoortige karakter aan sy pen-en-wastekeninge.
Hierdie eienskap word ook weerspieël in die helder kleure van sy skilderye.

Steenbok
Oil on canvas, 79 x 100 cm
SWA Central Government

Steinböckchen
Öl auf Tuch, 79 x 100 cm
SWA Zentrale Regierung

Steenbokke
Olie op doek, 79 x 100 cm
SWA Sentrale Regering

Black rhinoceros
Pen-and-wash, 24 x 36 cm
Coll. P Böttger, Windhoek

Spitzmaul-Nashorn
Feder- und Tuschezeichnung, 24 x 36 cm
Sammlung P Böttger, Windhoek

Swartrenoster
Getinte pentekening, 24 x 36 cm
Vers. P Böttger, Windhoek

Gemsbok
Pen-and-wash, 27 x 35 cm
Coll. W Böttger, Windhoek

Oryx-Antilope
Feder- und Tuschezeichnung, 27 x 35 cm
Sammlung W Böttger, Windhoek

Gemsbok
Getinte pentekening, 27 x 35 cm
Vers. W Böttger, Windhoek

2-4-66

**Lioness**
Pen-and-wash, 24 x 30 cm
Coll. B Theiss, Windhoek

**Löwin**
Feder- und Tuschezeichnung, 24 x 30 cm
Sammlung B Theiss, Windhoek

**Leeuwyfie**
Getinte pentekening, 24 x 30 cm
Vers. B Theiss, Windhoek

**Spotted hyena**
Pen-and-ink, 48 x 66 cm
Coll. J Jooste, Firgrove

**Gefleckte Hyänen**
Federzeichnung, 48 x 66 cm
Sammlung J Jooste, Firgrove

**Gevlekte hiënas**
Pentekening, 48 x 66 cm
Vers. J Jooste, Firgrove

## Fritz Krampe

Fritz Krampe was born in Berlin in 1913. He studied at the Akademie der Bildenden Künste in Berlin from 1931 to 1933, then at the Münchener Akademie, and from 1935 to 1939 he was a master-pupil at the Preussische Staatsakademie für Bildende Künste. His career as an artist was interrupted by World War II, during which he spent five years as a prisoner of war in Australia. After the war he lived and worked in Berlin, but in 1951 he emigrated to Cape Town. Shortly afterwards he settled in Windhoek and it was from there that he started his extensive travels that took him all over the African continent.

Although his portraits and illustrations are exceptional, his wildlife studies are his most striking works. Nature and its inexorable laws fascinated him. Depicted with great sensitivity and extraordinary vitality, his animals seem to explode from his enormous canvases. It was his keen interest in and his portrayal of wildlife that earned him the title of honorary game-warden of Etosha. During his visit to India in 1966, he was fatally injured by an elephant. In life and in death Krampe was as fearless as the untamed spirit that is reflected in his works.

Fritz Krampe wurde 1913 in Berlin geboren. Von 1931 bis 1933 studierte er an der Akademie der Bildenden Künste in Berlin, danach an der Münchener Akademie und von 1935 bis 1939 war er Meisterschüler an der Preussischen Staatsakademie für Bildende Künste. Durch den Ausbruch des Zweiten Weltkrieges und seiner fünfjährigen Kriegsgefangenschaft in Australien wurde seine Laufbahn als Künstler unterbrochen. Nach dem Krieg wohnte und arbeitete er wieder in Berlin. 1951 wanderte er nach Kapstadt aus. Er liess sich kurz danach in Windhoek nieder, seinem Ausgangspunkt zu den zahlreichen Reisen, die ihn über den ganzen afrikanischen Kontinent führten.

Obwohl seine Porträts und Illustrationen von ausserordentlicher Qualität sind, haben seine Darstellungen des Tierlebens die grössere Wirkung. Er war tief ergriffen von den unerbittlichen Naturgesetzen. Seine Tiere, mit grossem Einfühlungsvermögen und besonderer Lebenskraft dargestellt, brechen förmlich aus den riesigen Gemälden hervor. Auf Grund seines lebhaften Interesses am Wildleben und seiner Arbeiten über dieses Thema wurde er zum Ehrenwildhüter von Etoscha ernannt. Während seines Besuches in Indien 1966 wurde er von einem Elefanten tödlich verletzt. Im Leben wie im Tod war Krampe genauso furchtlos wie der ungezähmte Geist, der so stark aus seinen Werken spricht.

Fritz Krampe is in 1913 in Berlyn gebore. Hy studeer aan die Akademie der Bildenden Künste in Berlyn van 1931 tot 1933, daarna aan die Münchener Akademie, en van 1935 tot 1939 aan die Preussische Staatsakademie für Bildende Künste as meester-student. Sy loopbaan as kunstenaar word onderbreek deur die uitbreek van die Tweede Wêreldoorlog en 'n tydperk van vyf jaar as krygsgevangene in Australië. Ná die oorlog woon en werk hy weer in Berlyn. In 1951 emigreer hy na Kaapstad en vestig hom kort daarna in Windhoek. Dit was hiervandaan dat hy sy uitgebreide reise dwarsoor die vasteland van Afrika onderneem het.

Hoewel sy portrette en illustrasies van besondere gehalte getuig, is dit sy uitbeelding van die dierelewe wat die grootste trefkrag het. Hy is diep aangegryp deur die genadelose wette van die natuur. Sy diere, uitgebeeld met fyn aanvoeling en besondere lewenskragtigheid, bars te voorskyn uit enorme skilderye. Dit was sy groot belangstelling in die dierelewe en sy uitbeelding daarvan wat hom die titel van erewildbewaarder van Etosha besorg het. In 1966, tydens sy besoek aan Indië, word hy noodlottig beseer deur 'n olifant. In sy lewe en sterwe was Krampe net so vreesloos as die ongetemde gees wat so kragtig uit sy werke spreek.

**Blue wildebeest**
Water-colour, 50 x 73,5 cm
State Museum, Windhoek

**Streifengnus**
Aquarell, 50 x 73,5 cm
Staatsmuseum, Windhoek

**Blouwildebeeste**
Waterverf, 50 x 73,5 cm
Staatsmuseum, Windhoek

**Baboon**
Charcoal, 58 x 48 cm
Coll. P Strack, Windhoek

**Pavian**
Kohlezeichnung, 58 x 48 cm
Sammlung P Strack, Windhoek

**Bobbejaan**
Houtskooltekening, 58 x 48 cm
Vers. P Strack, Windhoek

**Wild dogs**
Brush drawing, 48 x 58 cm
Coll. P Strack, Windhoek

**Hyänenhunde**
Pinselzeichnung, 48 x 58 cm
Sammlung P Strack, Windhoek

**Wildehonde**
Kwastekening, 48 x 58 cm
Vers. P Strack, Windhoek

**Fighting zebra**
Brush drawing, 87 x 58 cm
Coll. S von Bach, Windhoek

**Kämpfende Zebras**
Pinselzeichnung, 87 x 58 cm
Sammlung S von Bach, Windhoek

**Vegtende sebras**
Kwastekening, 87 x 58 cm
Vers. S von Bach, Windhoek

**Giraffe**
Charcoal, 61,5 x 46,5 cm
Coll. HC de la Bat, Stellenbosch

**Giraffe**
Kohlezeichnung, 61,5 x 46,5 cm
Sammlung HC de la Bat, Stellenbosch

**Kameelperd**
Houtskooltekening, 61,5 x 46,5 cm
Vers. HC de la Bat, Stellenbosch

**Lion**
Crayon, 36 x 49 cm
Coll. HC de la Bat, Stellenbosch

**Löwe**
Kreidezeichnung, 36 x 49 cm
Sammlung HC de la Bat, Stellenbosch

**Leeumannetjie**
Kryttekening, 36 x 49 cm
Vers. HC de la Bat, Stellenbosch

## John Muafangejo

John Muafangejo was born in 1943 at Oshikango, near the Angolan border. In 1968, after training as a teacher at Oshikango, he enrolled as a student at the ELC Art & Craft Centre in Rorke's Drift, Natal, where he attended a two-year course in drawing, painting, graphic art, weaving and textile design. After his return to Owambo he taught at the St. Mary's Mission School at Odibo for some time. In 1974 he returned to Rorke's Drift for an additional one-year course.

He now works as a full-time artist in Windhoek and concentrates on lino- and woodcut and tapestry design. His subject matters are animals, traditional Wambo life, religious themes and his own experiences.

John Muafangejo wurde 1943 in Oshikango in der Nähe der angolanischen Grenze geboren. Nach seiner Ausbildung als Lehrer in Oshikango liess er sich im Jahre 1968 als Student am **ELC Art & Craft Centre** in Rorkes Drift, Natal, einschreiben, wo er zwei Jahre lang Malerei, Graphik, Weben und Textilentwurf studierte. Er kehrte nach Owambo zurück und unterrichtete eine Zeit lang an der St. Mary Missionsschule in Odibo. Im Jahre 1974 kehrte er zu einem weiteren Studienjahr nach Rorkes Drift zurück.

Er arbeitet jetzt als freischaffender Künstler in Windhoek und beschäftigt sich hauptsächlich mit der Linol- und Holzschnittkunst und mit Tapisserie-Entwurf. Die Gegenstände seiner Arbeiten umfassen Tiere, das traditionelle Stammesleben, religiöse Themen und seine eigenen Lebenserfahrungen.

John Muafangejo is in 1943 te Oshikango, naby die Angolagrens, gebore. Ná sy opleiding as onderwyser op Oshikango, skryf hy hom in 1968 in as student aan die ELC Art & Craft Centre te Rorke's Drift, Natal, waar hy vir twee jaar opleiding ondergaan in teken-, skilder- en grafiese kuns, weef en tekstielontwerp. Met sy terugkeer na Owambo gee hy 'n ruk lank klas aan die St. Mary-sendingskool te Odibo. In 1974 gaan hy weer na Rorke's Drift vir 'n verdere jaar van studie.

Hy woon nou in Windhoek as voltydse kunstenaar en spits hom veral toe op lino- en houtsneekuns en tapisserie-ontwerp. Hy verbeeld diere, die tradisionele Wambo-lewe, religieuse temas en sy lewenservarings.

Etosha Pan wildlife
Lino-cut, 44 x 70 cm
Coll. artist

Wilde Tiere der Etoschapfanne
Linolschnitt, 44 x 70 cm
Sammlung Künstler

Wilde diere van Etoshapan
Linosnee, 44 x 70 cm
Vers. kunstenaar

"Elephant is killing a lion in
funny way in 1975"
Lino-cut, 45 x 34 cm
Coll. artist

Elefant, der einen Löwen 1975 auf
komische Art und Weise tötet
Linolschnitt, 45 x 34 cm
Sammlung Künstler

Olifant wat 'n leeu op snaakse
wyse dood in 1975
Linosnee, 45 x 34 cm
Vers. kunstenaar

## Heinz Pulon

Heinz Pulon was born in Windhoek in 1930 and received his early art instruction from Helmut Lewin and Professor Otto Schröder. After initial training as a carpenter, he enrolled at the Akademie der Bildenden Künste in Munich in 1951.
Having completed his studies, he returned to Windhoek where he held his first exhibition. In 1958 he returned to Munich for a further year of study. He then spent some years criss-crossing Angola, Zambia and Botswana as a safari leader and professional hunter before settling as a full-time artist in Windhoek in 1973. He was made an honorary game-warden in recognition of his involvement in wildlife conservation. His love of birds and animals is reflected in his superb etchings.

Heinz Pulon wurde 1930 in Windhoek geboren. Seinen ersten Kunstunterricht empfing er von Helmut Lewin und Professor Otto Schröder. Nach seiner anfänglichen Tischlerlehre liess er sich 1951 als Student an der Akademie der Bildenden Künste in München einschreiben. Nach Abschluss seines Studiums kehrte er nach Windhoek zurück, wo er seine erste Ausstellung hielt. 1958 ging er für ein weiteres Studienjahr nach München. Danach durchkreuzte er Angola, Sambia und Botswana als Safarileiter und Berufsjäger. 1973 liess er sich als freischaffender Künstler in Windhoek nieder. In Anerkennung für seinen Einsatz für den Wildschutz wurde er zum Ehrenwildhüter ernannt. Seine Liebe zum Vogel- und Tierleben spiegelt sich in seinen ausgezeichneten Radierungen wider.

Heinz Pulon is in 1930 in Windhoek gebore. Hy ontvang sy vroeë kunsonderrig van Helmut Lewin en professor Otto Schröder. Ná sy aanvanklike opleiding as skrynwerker, skryf hy hom in as student aan die Akademie der Bildenden Künste te München in 1951. Na afloop van sy studie, keer hy terug na Windhoek en hou sy eerste uitstalling hier. In 1958 keer hy terug na München vir 'n verdere jaar van studie. Hierna deurkruis hy Angola, Zambië en Botswana as safari-leier en professionele jagter. In 1973 keer hy terug en vestig hom as heeltydse kunstenaar in Windhoek. Weens sy betrokkenheid by natuurbewaring, word hy vereer met 'n toekenning as erewildbewaarder. Sy voorliefde vir die voël- en dierelewe word weerspieël in sy uitmuntende etse.

Leopard
Coloured etching, 16,5 x 13 cm
Coll. S Thalmaier, Windhoek

Leopard
Farbige Radierung, 16,5 x 13 cm
Sammlung S Thalmaier, Windhoek

Luiperd
Gekleurde ets, 16,5 x 13 cm
Vers. S Thalmaier, Windhoek

Orig.Paol. 7/6 #3                    Heinz Meulen 86

**Bateleur eagle**
Coloured etching, 10,5 x 17,5 cm
Coll. artist

**Gaukler**
Farbige Radierung, 10,5 x 17,5 cm
Sammlung Künstler

**Berghaan**
Gekleurde ets, 10,5 x 17,5 cm
Vers. kunstenaar

Arendroof.   4/6                                    Henry Raeburn
                                                            80

**Sable antelope**
Etching, 14,5 x 14,5 cm
Coll. artist

**Säbelantilope**
Radierung, 14,5 x 14,5 cm
Sammlung Künstler

**Swartwitpens**
Ets, 14,5 x 14,5 cm
Vers. kunstenaar

Oniegkael.  6/6.                    Hengprukes  86

**Elephant**
Pencil-and-wash, 32 x 25 cm
Coll. artist

**Elefant**
Bleistift- und Tuschezeichnung, 32 x 25 cm
Sammlung Künstler

**Olifant**
Getinte potloodtekening, 32 x 25 cm
Vers. kunstenaar

## Joachim Voigts

Joachim Voigts was born in Windhoek in 1907, but went to school in Germany. He took a course in graphic art at Braunschweig and studied at the Landeskunstschule in Hamburg from 1928 to 1930. After four years as a commercial artist in Windhoek, he continued his studies at the Akademie der Bildenden Künste in Munich. He has since been living and working on his farm in the Okahandja district.

He is a regular visitor to Etosha and has gained renown especially for his excellent woodcuts with wildlife motifs. He is also known for his illustrations in many educational books and for his trilingual children's book SWA Fables of which he is the author and illustrator.

Joachim Voigts wurde 1907 in Windhoek geboren. In Deutschland ging er zur Schule. Danach belegte er einen Graphik-Kurs in Braunschweig. Von 1928 bis 1930 studierte er an der Landeskunstschule in Hamburg. Nach vier Jahren als Gebrauchsgraphiker in Windhoek setzte er sein Studium an der Akademie der Bildenden Künste in München fort. Seitdem wohnt und arbeitet er auf seiner Farm im Okahandja-Bezirk.

Er besucht regelmässig die Etoschapfanne und machte sich vor allem mit seinen ausgezeichneten Holzschnitten mit Tiermotiven einen Namen. Der Künstler ist ebenfalls für die Illustration zahlreicher Schulbücher, sowie für das dreisprachige Kinderbuch SWA Fabeln bekannt, beim letztgenannten als Autor und Illustrator zugleich.

Joachim Voigts is in 1907 in Windhoek gebore maar ontvang sy skoolopleiding in Duitsland. Hierna volg hy 'n kursus in grafiese kuns te Braunschweig. Van 1928 tot 1930 studeer hy aan die Landeskunstschule in Hamburg. Ná vier jaar as handelskunstenaar in Windhoek, sit hy sy studies in München voort aan die Akademie der Bildenden Künste. Hierna woon en werk hy op sy plaas in die Okahandja-distrik.

Hy is 'n gereelde besoeker aan Etosha en het bekendheid verwerf veral vir sy voortreflike houtsneë met dierelewe as motief. Hy is ook bekend vir sy illustrasies in talle opvoedkundige boeke asook vir sy drietalige kinderboek, SWA Fabels, waarvan hy die outeur en illustreerder is.

Secretary bird killing snake
Woodcut, 22 x 28 cm
Coll. artist

Sekretär tötet eine Schlange
Holzschnitt, 22 x 28 cm
Sammlung Künstler

Sekretarisvoël wat slang doodmaak
Houtsnee, 22 x 28 cm
Vers. kunstenaar

**Gemsbok**
Woodcut, 26 x 25 cm
Coll. artist

**Oryx-Antilopen**
Holzschnitt, 26 x 25 cm
Sammlung Künstler

**Gemsbokke**
Houtsnee, 26 x 25 cm
Vers. kunstenaar

Porcupine
Woodcut, 22 x 28 cm
Coll. artist

Stachelschwein
Holzschnitt, 22 x 28 cm
Sammlung Künstler

Ystervark
Houtsnee, 22 x 28 cm
Vers. kunstenaar

**Guinea fowl**
Woodcut, 17 x 21,5 cm
Coll. N Wagner, Stellenbosch

**Perlhühner**
Holzschnitt, 17 x 21,5 cm
Sammlung N Wagner, Stellenbosch

**Tarentale**
Houtsnee, 17 x 21,5 cm
Vers. N Wagner, Stellenbosch

JOVO